CONTENTS

The Deer

The deer has been an all-time favorite subject of wildlife artists throughout the ages.

The deer's graceful lines and genteel manner make for an interesting subject, not just for the viewer, but for the carver as well. Unfortunately, the graceful lines and thin legs and hooves of the deer also make it an intimidating subject for carvers of all skill levels. Knowing your subject thoroughly can help allay your fears and remove your reservations.

I will describe the white-tailed deer here. Before you start carving, you'll want to do some additional research on your own. Start with books and videos at your local library and online. Museums and zoos are also good places to find reference material. Remember, though, that taxidermists who make museum models can sometimes make mistakes if they are not familiar with the animal. Also remember that zoo animals never exactly resemble their wild counterparts. Most are better fed and better groomed than deer in the wild.

The white-tailed deer is the most abundant hoofed mammal in North America. It lives in mixed woodlands, in second growth forests, and at the forest's edge. In the summer, adults' coats are tawny on the top with white on the bottom of the head, neck, belly, and tail. In winter, adults' coats change to grayish-brown on top. The white-tailed deer is the only eastern deer with a tail that is white below and the same color as the back above. The antlers of the white-tailed deer have erect, unbranched tines arising from a main base.

There are species of deer other than the white-tailed deer, of course, such as the mule deer, the red deer, and many others that vary widely in shape, color, and size. This book focuses on white-tailed deer, but plenty of the information is applicable to other species. Just make sure if you decide to carve a different species than the white-tailed deer to do your research beforehand.

PLANNING TO CARVE A DEER

After you have chosen a species of deer to carve and have researched the animal thoroughly, it is time to plan your carving. Once again, I must stress that it is important to understand the animal before you attempt to carve it. Understanding the animal will help you adapt your sculpture to the wood's grain. You'll be able to match the bends of the deer with the bends of the wood and better capture the essence of the animal.

Remember, too, that each deer has its own personality and its own features. Like us, some have long noses, wide noses, wide-set eyes, or large ears. Also remember that everything about your deer will play a part in your carving. Is it winter or summer? Coats change color from season to season. Is it spring or fall? Antlers will be velvety in the spring; in the fall, they will be bony, and the buck's neck will be thicker and more muscled in order to support their weight. Was it a bad winter? If so, your deer will be thin.

You will find that the project and patterns in this book are designed to make you work on studying your subject. The step-by-step project will help you carve a walking buck. The patterns include a buck bust, a doe with a fawn, and two different fawn designs. Each pattern has multiple views to help you with any redesign you wish to do. Don't be afraid to use a photocopier to enlarge or reduce a pattern.

You can also redraw patterns to create a walking deer by using the walking illustrations (page 35). The illustrations show how a deer's joints move when it walks. Notice how the shoulder moves up when it is supporting the weight. The same thing happens with the hips. The leg also shifts under the body when it is supporting the weight. One of the illustrations shows how the backbone, which is fused with the pelvis, moves along with the pelvis whenever the animal moves. Another illustration shows how the pelvis shifts right along with the step. The deer's shoulders are not fused to the backbone, but they are connected to it by tendons and ligaments and will move with a turn or weight shift. See how important anatomy is to planning your carving?

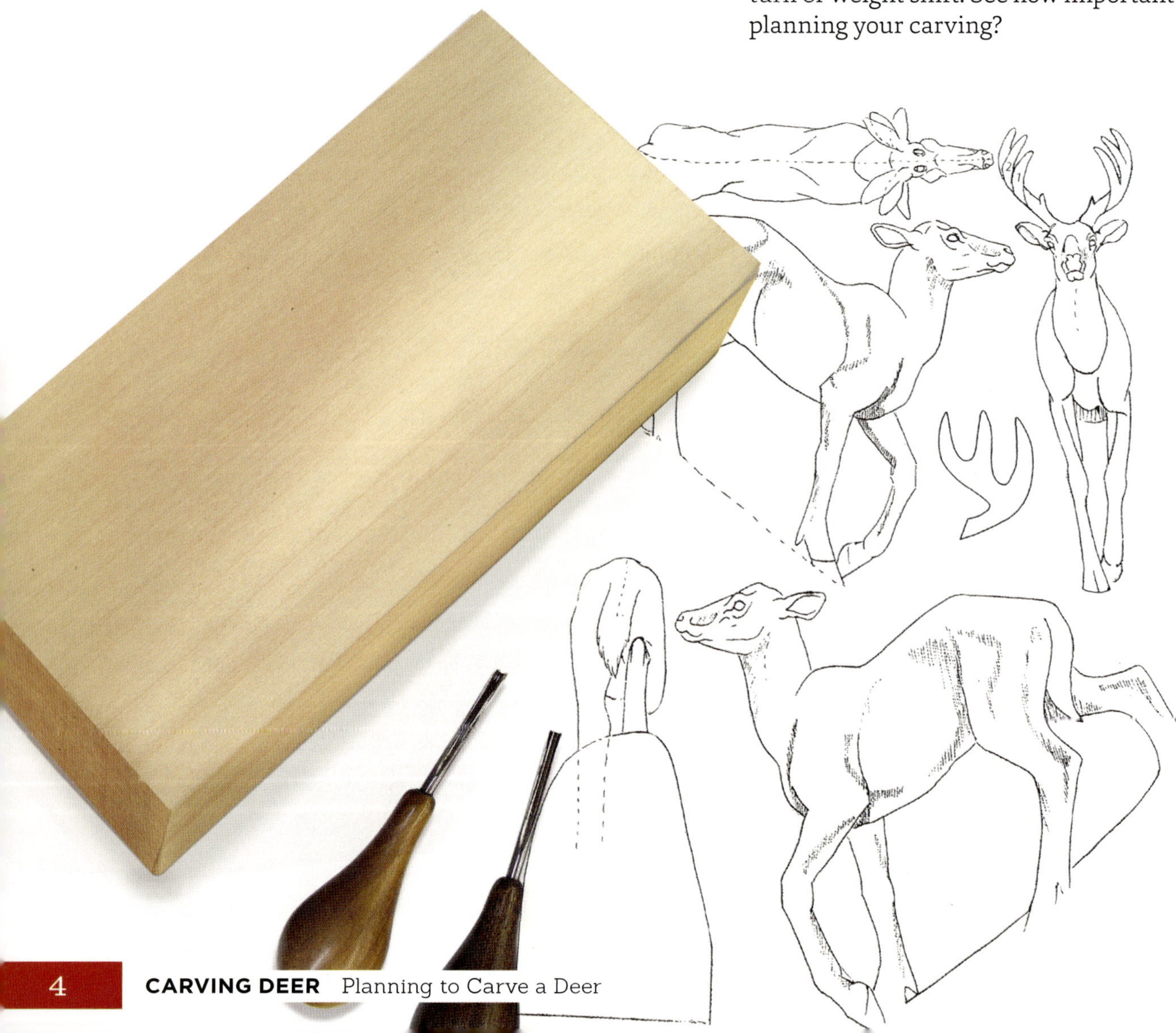

TOOLS

With any project I do, I use the tools that are best for me and for the wood. If the carving lends itself to hand tools, I use them. If power tools make more sense, I use them. Use whatever tools you feel most comfortable with; there is never only one way to do a project.

Whenever I teach, I always try to keep in mind that what may be important to me may not be important to my students or my readers. If you don't like woodburning or painting, don't do it. My objective is always to communicate the carving, texturing, burning, and painting aspects of what I do. Take what you like, and leave what you don't. I always aim to show you what I do so you can adapt some aspect of what I've presented to fit your needs.

Hand Tools

I use a lot of large and small palm tools, knives, and chisels. I prefer Denny Palm Tools and Drake Knives. When I'm carving wildlife projects, I most commonly use #6, #7, and #9 gouges and a detail knife. In the step-by-step project, I used a detail knife, a ¼" (6mm) #7 gouge and a ⅜" (10mm) #7 gouge.

Power Carving Tools

For power carving, I use Foredom and Wecheer rotary power carvers with ruby and diamond bits in various shapes, such as flame, bud, ball, and cylinder. Depending on the brand and the kind of rotary carver you buy, you often get a kit that contains bits and cutters. These aren't usually the best for carving, so I suggest looking around and purchasing the bits you need.

I also sometimes use reciprocating carvers like Proxxon and Arbortech, which are great for people with less hand strength. Ryobi also made reciprocating carvers that were great; although they no longer distribute them, you can find them new and used online. I use Flexcut blades with these tools.

Woodburning Tools

The woodburner I use is a Detail Master, but you can texture your carving with any woodburner that has an adjustable thermostat. I have lots of different tips for the various parts of the animal. You'll find that there are many burner tips available on the market. I commonly use skew, microskew, spear, and rounded tips, but you'll want to experiment with others on your own.

Painting Tools

While there are many different ways to paint carvings, especially wildlife carvings, I regularly use acrylic paint. I don't stick to one brand; I like to buy what is on sale at the time! I suggest having lots of different brushes available for painting; however, I almost always use a stiff-bristled brush, a detail brush, and a soft round brush on my carvings.

Hand Carve a Majestic Buck

Materials:

- Basswood, 3" (76mm) thick: 5¾" x 6½" (146mm x 165mm)
- Basswood, 2" (51mm) thick: antlers, 1" x 1½" (25mm x 38mm)
- Acrylic paint: nutmeg brown, black, dull white, golden brown
- Low-gloss tung oil or a finish of your choice

Tools:

- #7 gouges: ⅜" (10mm), ¼" (6mm)
- Rotary power carver with flame-shaped ruby bit
- Detail knife
- Woodburner with tips: microskew
- Paintbrushes: Blick studio bristle #5 soft, Blick #5660 detailer, wide soft-bristled brush

With this project, I wanted to create a majestic look that captures the deer's graceful movements. To accomplish this, I posed the deer walking down a sloped base.

I enjoy carving deer because, even if you use the same general pose, you can give the deer a different attitude by changing the positions of the ears. If you choose to make the project a doe instead of a buck, slim down the features of the body.

In this demonstration, I'll insert the antlers before beginning the woodburning process. If I were to carve the project again, I'd burn the piece first rather than working around the antlers. This way, I wouldn't have to worry about breaking the antlers.

Start by tracing the left side-view pattern (page 16) onto the blank. Cut the profile with a band saw. Trace the top, back, front, and right side view of the deer onto the blank. Leave extra wood around the legs so you can change the pose of the legs as needed.

Carve the deer and base from a single piece of wood. The antlers are carved separately for added strength.

1 **Rough out the side view of the deer.** Use a ⅜" (10mm) #7 gouge. Leave extra wood around the legs and face. Draw the legs and underbelly on both sides. Shade the areas to remove.

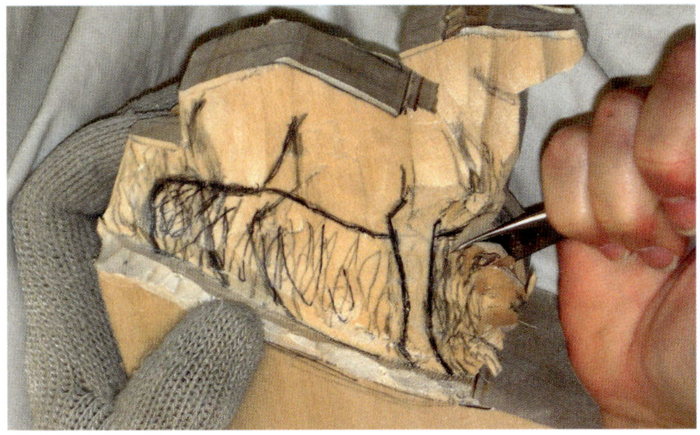

2 **Remove the extra wood around the legs.** Use the ⅜" (10mm) #7 gouge to remove the shaded areas. Carve away half of each of the four legs.

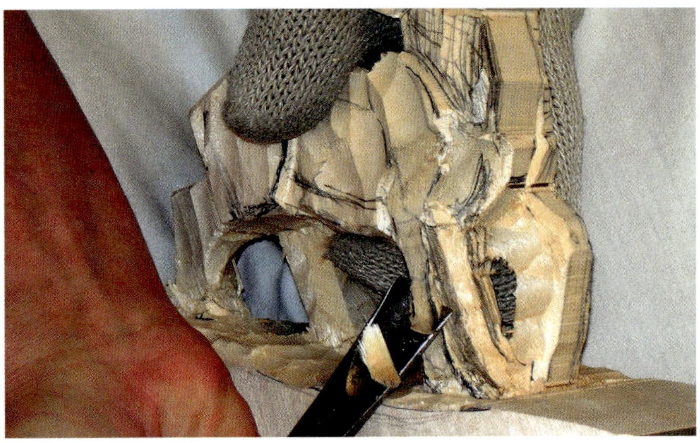

3 **Rough out the legs and neck.** Draw the shapes of the legs and neck. Carve away the extra wood with the ⅜" (10mm) #7 gouge.

4 **Rough out the shoulders, hips, and knees.** Mark the areas to remove. Carve away the extra wood with the ⅜" (10mm) #7 gouge.

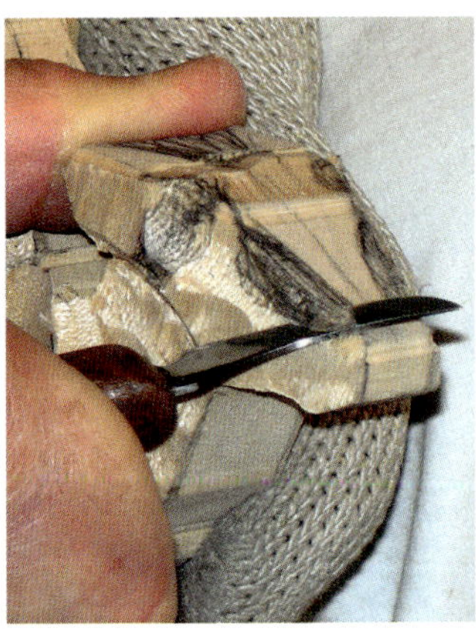

5 **Carve the bridge of the nose, eye sockets, and ears.** Use a detail knife to remove the wood along the nose and at the base of the ears. Use a ¼" (6mm) #7 gouge to carve the eye sockets and the area between the ears.

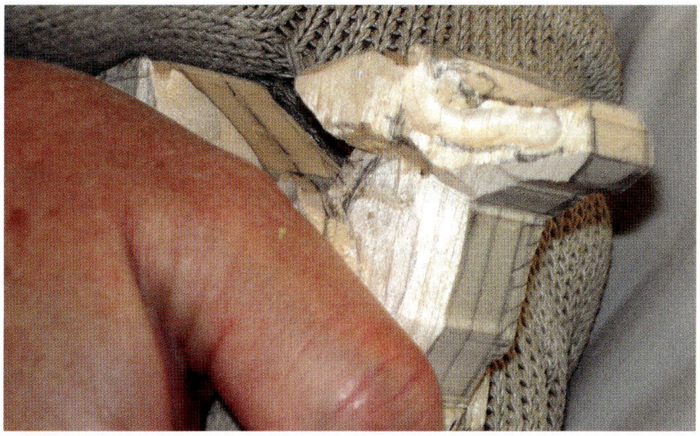

6 **Carve the cheekbones.** Draw the cheek areas. Carve away the extra wood with the ¼" (6mm) #7 gouge. The eye areas should protrude a bit. Taper the area under the jaw with the detail knife.

7 **Carve the shoulders.** Mark the angles and shapes of the shoulders. Carve these areas with the ⅜" (10mm) #7 gouge.

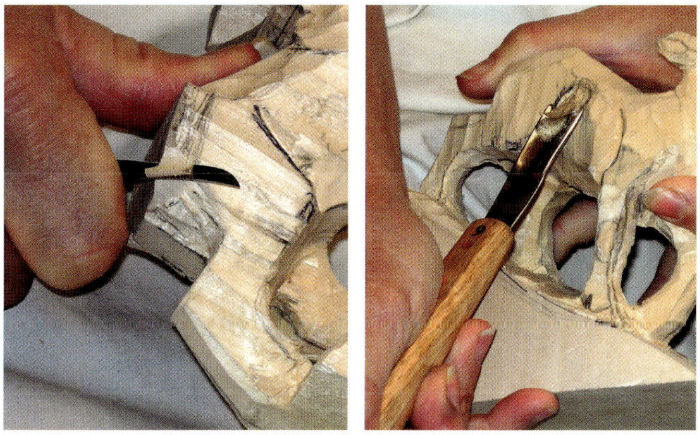

8 **Carve the pelvis.** Carve the pelvis and rump area with the detail knife. Then, carve the lower back with the ⅜" (10mm) #7 gouge.

Buck: Adding the Details

9 **Carve the eyes.** Draw the eyes. Stop-cut along the eye lines with the detail knife. Carve away small inverted pyramids for the tear ducts. Remove the excess wood in front of the eyeballs, and undercut each eyeball to make it look round.

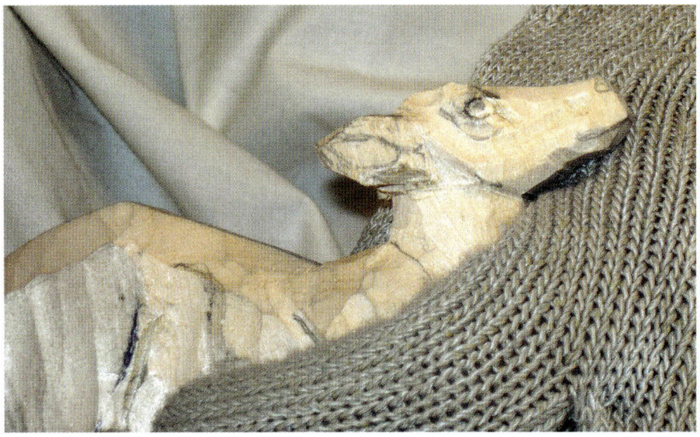

10 **Carve the mouth and jaw.** Draw the mouth and make a stop cut along the line. Shape the chin area, and refine the bottom jaw where it meets the neck.

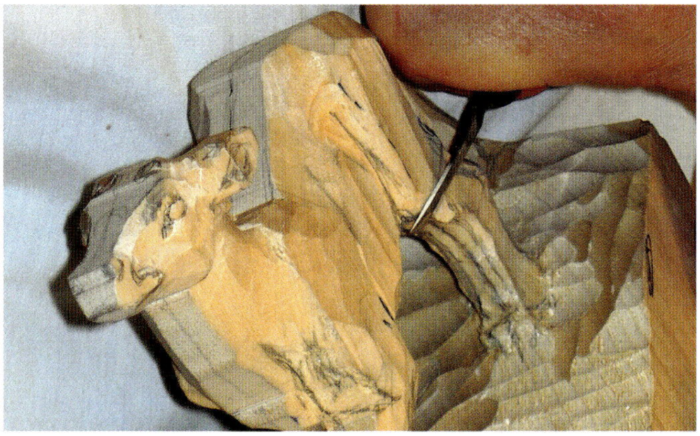

11 **Start shaping the legs.** Mark a centerline on the front side of the back leg. Then, mark the bend in the knee, the upper leg, and the Achilles tendon. Carve down at an angle from the centerline mark, which is the highest part on the leg.

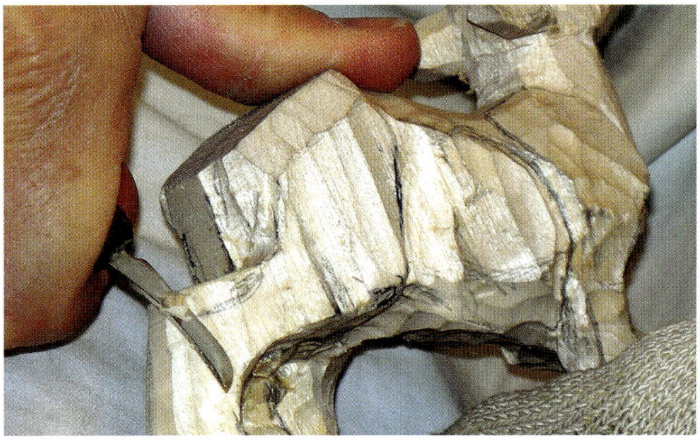

12 **Finish shaping the legs.** Cut at an angle from the bend in the knee to the upper leg. Then carve at an angle toward the Achilles tendon. You want a slight hollow on either side of the tendon. Use the same techniques to carve the other legs. The legs should end up roughly diamond-shaped.

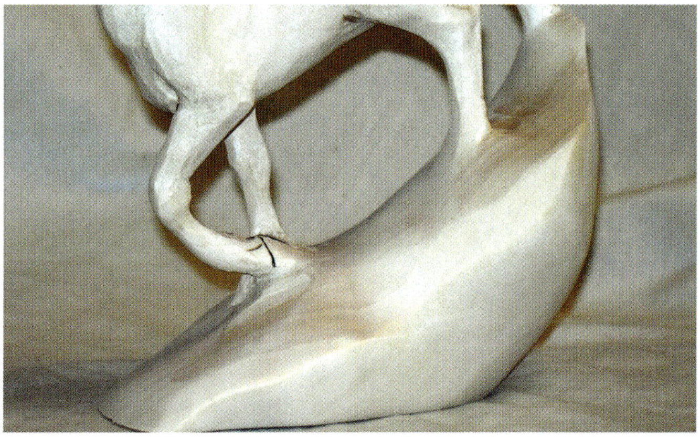

13 **Shape the base.** Round the hard angles of the base, and carve it into an interesting shape, if desired. I wanted the base to imitate a path on a hill, so I carved wavy edges. I also left some wood around the hooves so I could texture and paint those areas later.

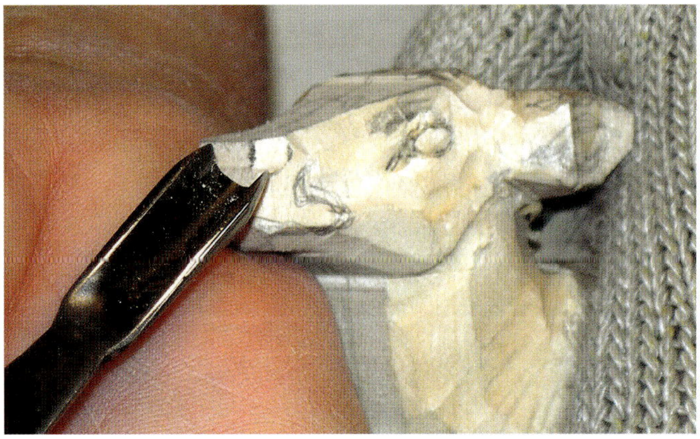

14 **Carve the nose and ears.** Draw the nose and the hollows of the ears. Carve both areas with the ¼" (6mm) #7 gouge. Use the detail knife to remove the gouge marks and round any rough areas on the deer. You may also use a flame-shaped ruby bit in a rotary power carver or sandpaper.

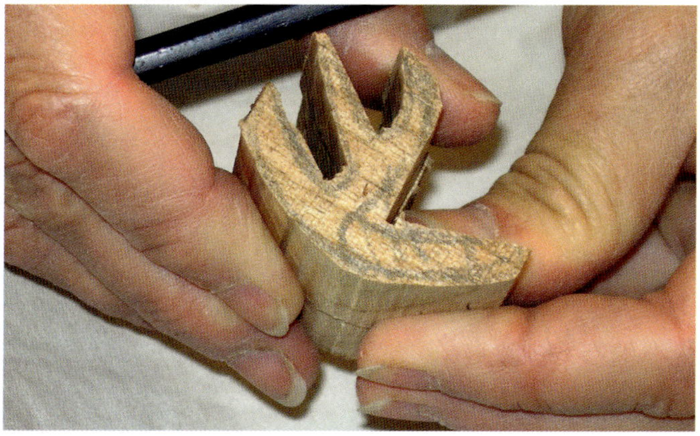

15 **Cut the antler blanks.** Trace the pattern onto a 2" (51mm)-thick blank. Cut along the lines with a band saw. Then, cut the antler blank in half. Draw the front-view pattern onto the antlers.

16 **Carve the antlers.** Remove the excess wood with a knife. If you want the buck's antlers to look like they are in velvet for a spring or summer look, leave the antlers thick. For a fall buck, reduce the thickness of the antlers with a flame-shaped ruby bit in a rotary power carver.

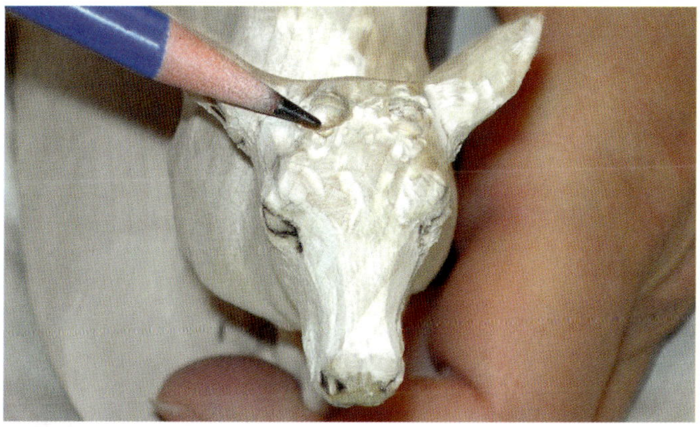

17 **Drill the holes for the antlers.** Mark the area to drill using the pattern as a guide. Carefully remove the wood to make a hole with a flame-shaped ruby bit in a rotary power carver. Be careful not to damage the head.

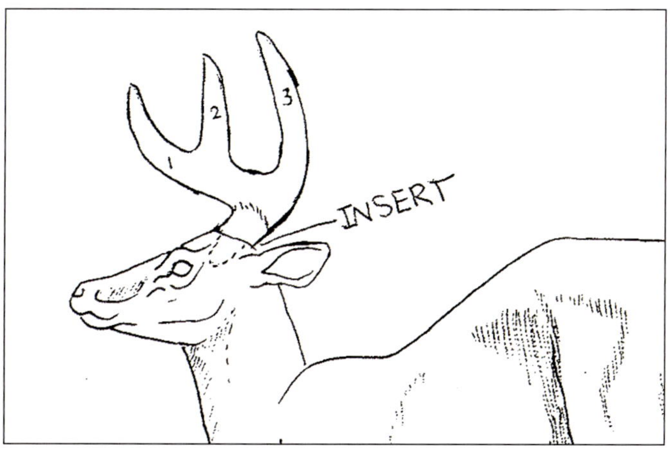

Creating Antlers

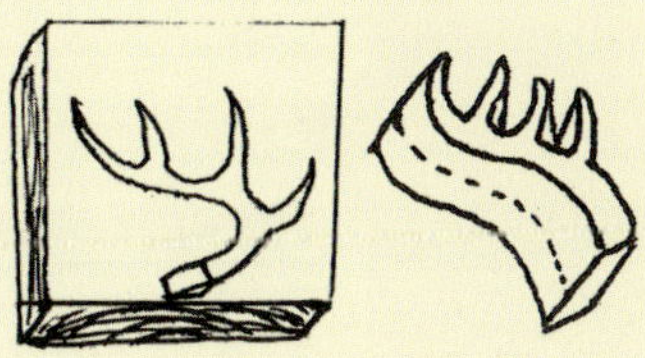

Cut out two side-view antlers with a scroll saw or band saw, or cut out one double-thick antler and saw it in half.

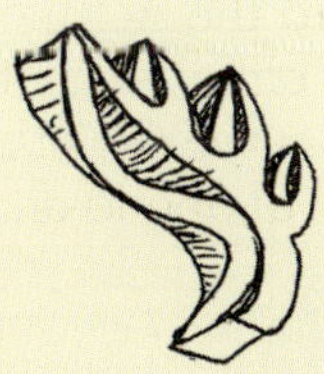

Draw the front view of the antlers onto the wood before beginning to shape them, and then remove unwanted wood with a large round burr. Brace the antler against wood or a hard surface (not a slick one) and take your time on each tine. For final shaping, use abrasives.

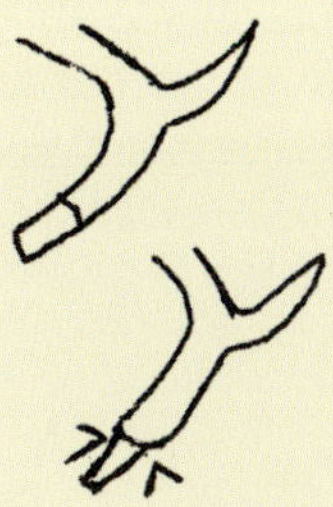

When finished, insert the elongated bases of the antlers into sockets drilled in the head. Glue them in place with wood glue. Make sure the right and left antlers are inserted on the correct sides.

Buck: Woodburning the Texture

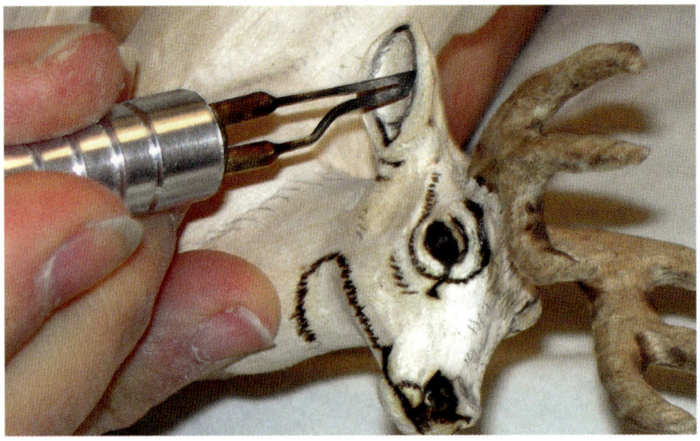

18 **Burn the facial features.** Draw the facial features. Trace along the features with a microskew tip. Burnish the eyes, nose, and inside the ears with the side of the microskew. Use the tip of a flame-shaped ruby bit in a rotary carver to texture the base where the deer's hooves meet the base. Outline the textured area with the microskew.

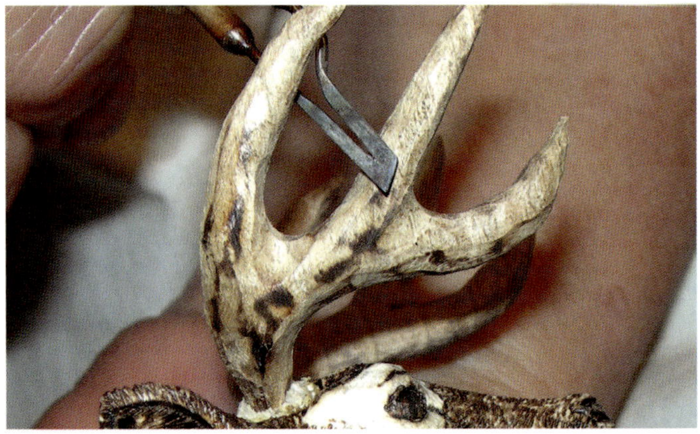

19 **Burn the rest of the fur texture.** Use the hair tract patterns as a guide. Then, draw the front hooves and the dew claw on the raised leg. Trace along these lines with the microskew tip. Glue the antlers in place. Burnish the hooves and antlers with the side of the microskew tip.

Steps continued on page 15.

Texturing with Woodburning Tools

Tips

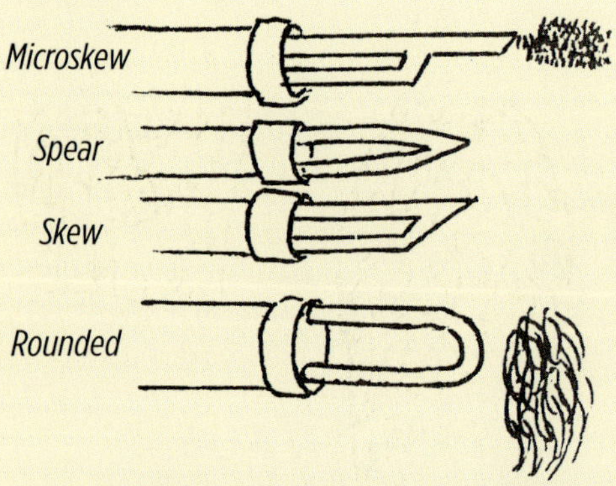

Press and pull the tool in the direction of the hair. Cross over softly. Use a stab-pull motion for short hairs.

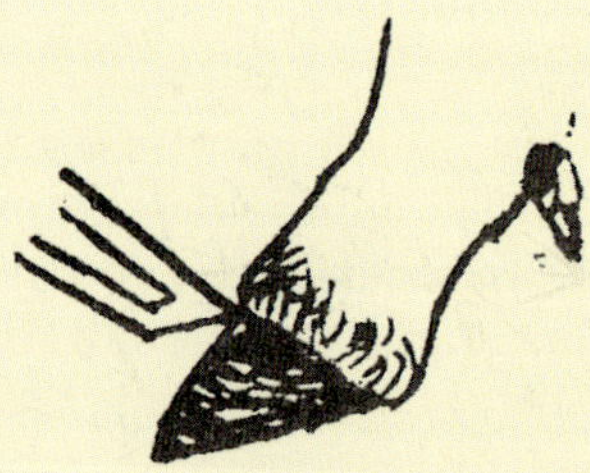

Use the same technique for hooves and dewclaws as you use for the eyes.

For the eyes, use the point of the woodburning tip along the outside of the eyeball. Then, with the flat side, burnish the sphere of the eyeball. To burnish the eyeball, use the lowest heat setting possible to smooth and flatten the wood fibers. Use this technique for the nose and the inside of the ears.

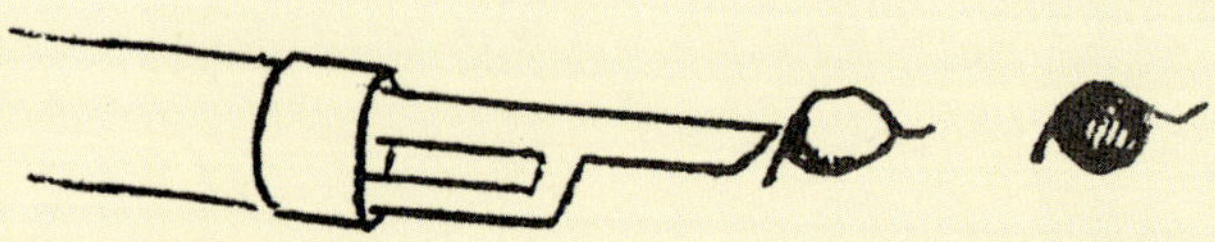

Hair Tract

Before painting, study the colors of the deer and be aware of what time of year it is in your carving. Most animals, including deer, have grayish-brown coats in winter so they blend in with the snowy landscape. Summer coats are rich and reddish in color to blend in with the summer foliage.

There are many styles of painting. Wildlife artists use a wide variety of mediums, including watercolors, oils, acrylic paints, colored pencils, markers, and stains. I regularly use acrylic paints and will focus on that medium here.

Because acrylics dry fast, I find that mixing the colors for each part of the body just before I want to paint that area works best. Mixing acrylics is easy. First, put the chosen color on your palette. Then, fill your brush with water and touch the brush to the paint. Mix the paint and the water to achieve a milky consistency, and apply it like a stain. I usually paint in the following order: head first, then neck, shoulders, front legs, body, back legs, and last, the tail.

Know where your light source is coming from. What areas of your carving will be in shadow and what areas will be hit by light? You'll want to darken the shadowed areas by adding a small amount of black to the base color. Brighten light areas by adding a small amount of white.

After I basecoat a carving, I often dry-brush paint over it to add a hint of color. Dry-brushing will show the texture you created through carving and woodburning. To dry-brush, scrub a small amount of paint into a stiff-bristled brush and apply the paint lightly to a dried area. Pull the brush gently in the opposite direction of the hair. In addition to highlighting the texture in a carving, dry-brushing can also set off areas the sun would hit on the animal.

When the deer is colored completely, use up the leftover paints on the base of the carving so the deer blends with its habitat. Mammals generally do! By using your leftover colors in this way, you can be sure the colors in your deer match the colors in the habitat perfectly. Plus, this wastes less paint.

An example of a reddish summer coat.

An example of a grayish-brown winter coat.

20 **Basecoat the white areas.** Thin white acrylic paint with water. Apply a base coat of the mixture to the eye areas, neck, chin, underbelly, and tail area with a #5 soft-bristled brush.

21 **Basecoat the brown areas.** Thin nutmeg brown acrylic paint with water and use the #5 soft-bristled brush to basecoat the brown areas, including the areas where the hooves meet the base. Paint the antlers with the thinned brown paint. Let the paint dry thoroughly.

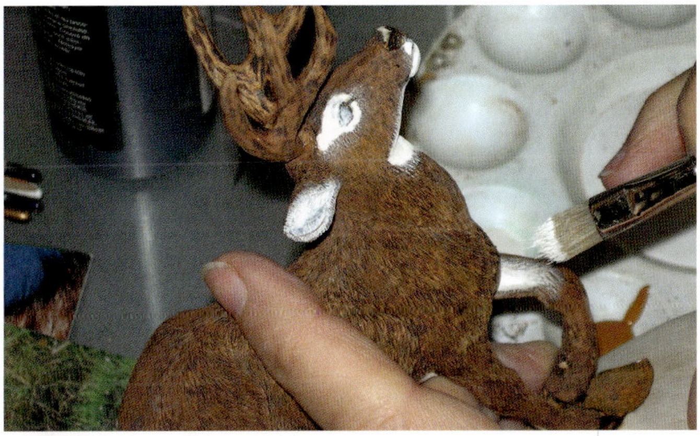

22 **Dry-brush the white areas and the antlers.** Dip a wide soft-bristled brush lightly into undiluted white acrylic paint. Scrub the tip of the brush on the palette and lightly touch the bristles over the white areas to add subtle highlights. Use the same technique to dry-brush the antlers.

23 **Dry-brush the brown areas.** Mix white with golden brown acrylic paint until you have a light brown color. Use the same technique explained in step 22 to dry-brush this mixture over the brown areas. Do not use this mixture on the antlers.

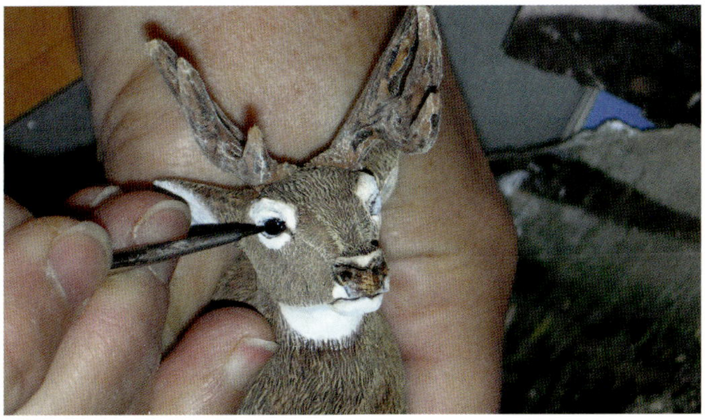

24 **Paint the black areas.** Apply undiluted black paint to the eyes, nose, and hooves with a detail brush. Use the same brush to paint the mouth and dewclaw. When dry, apply a clear finish of your choice. I use a low-gloss tung oil, but lacquer or polyurethane will work, as well.

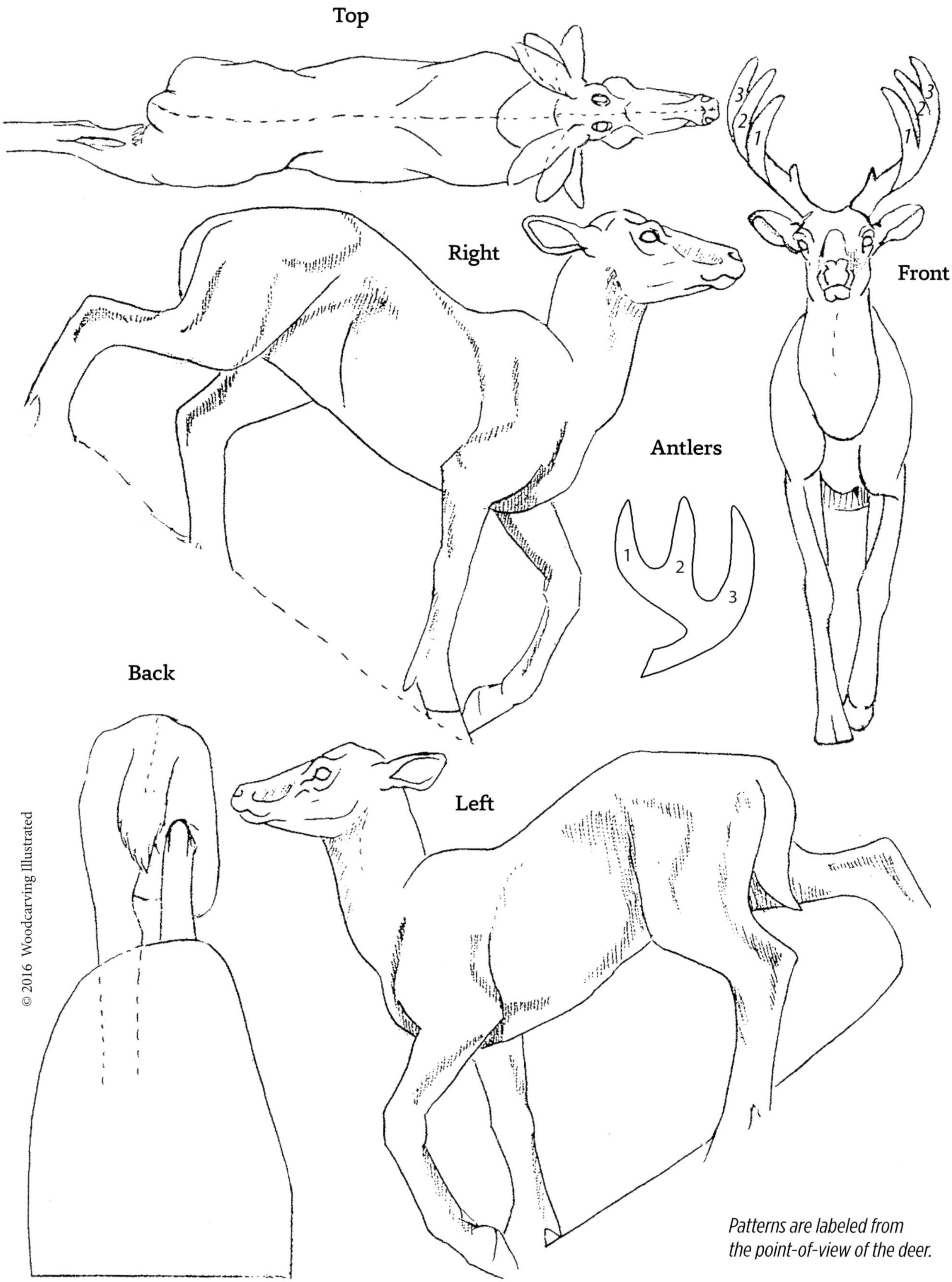

Patterns are labeled from the point-of-view of the deer.

Patterns

You can generalize the instructions in the majestic buck step-by-step to carve the projects in this section. The Appendix also has information on parts of the deer that can be more difficult to carve, as well as tips for tweaking these patterns. It is my hope that you'll be inspired to not only carve these projects, but also to capture the deer in different ages, times of year, stances, and positions.

White-Tailed Deer Bust

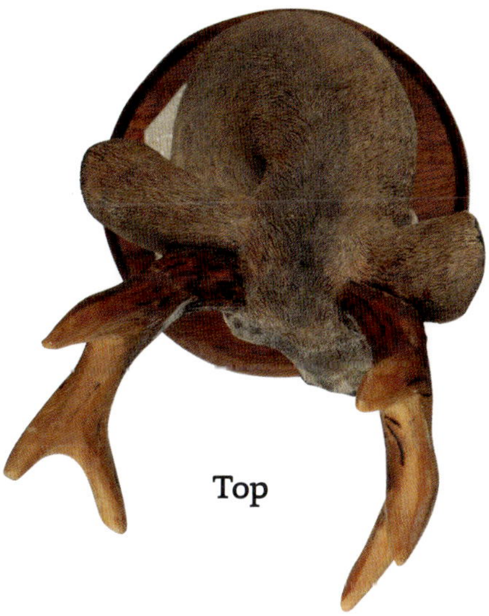

Top

Carving Reference

Front

Back

Right

Left

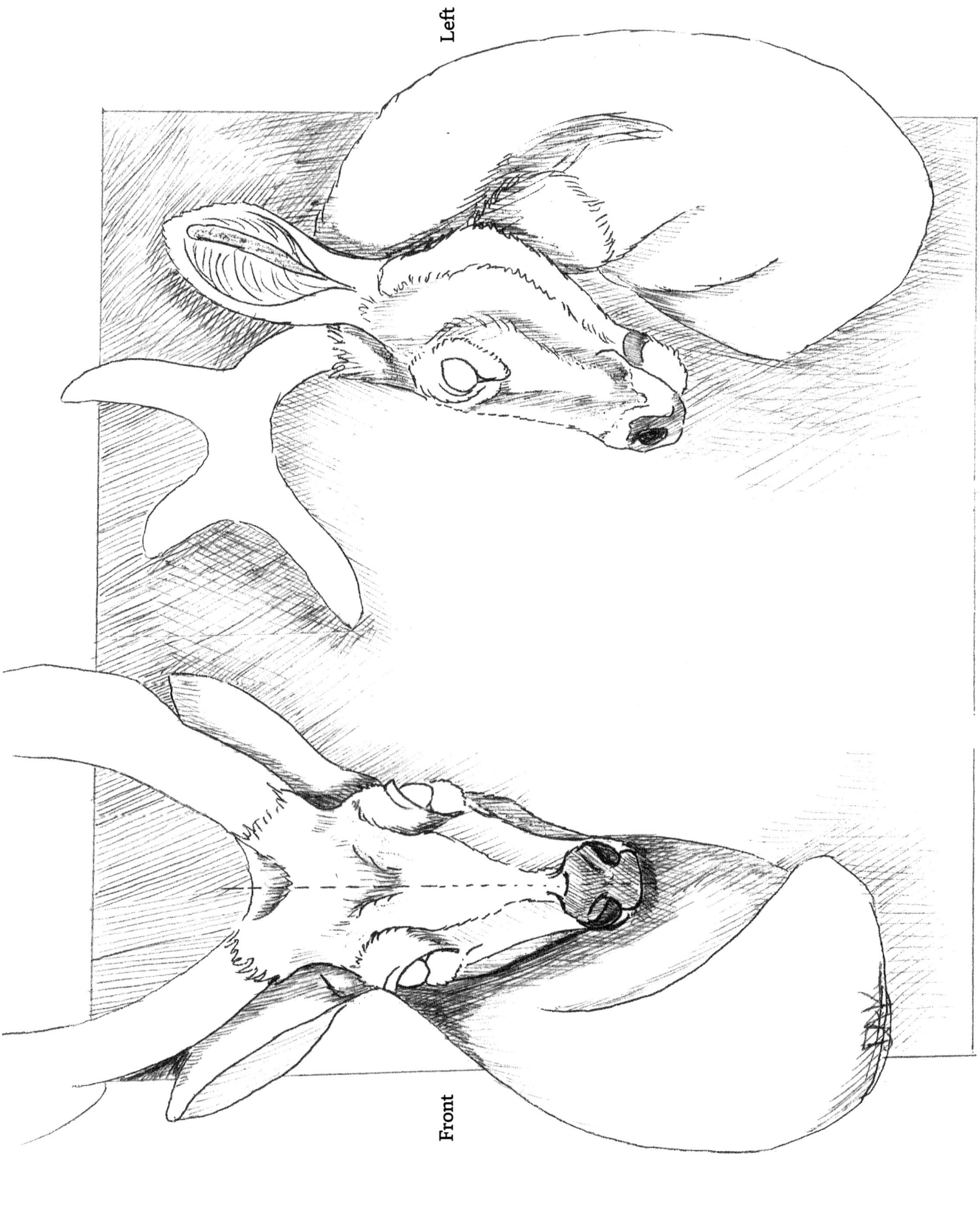
Left
Front

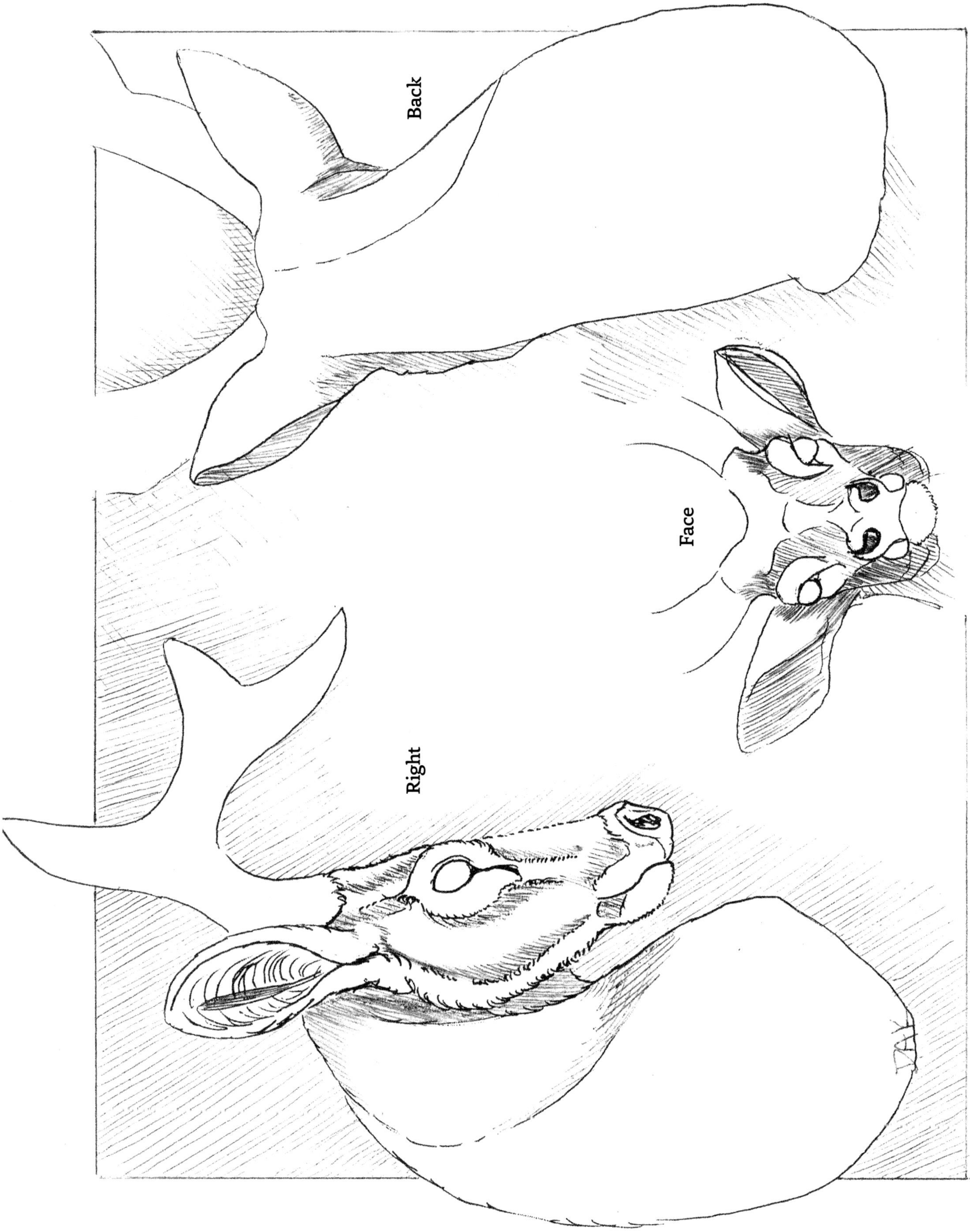
Back
Face
Right

Hair Tract

TWO FAWNS

Carving Reference

Right

Left

Back

Front

Top

Front
Head
Top
Right

Left

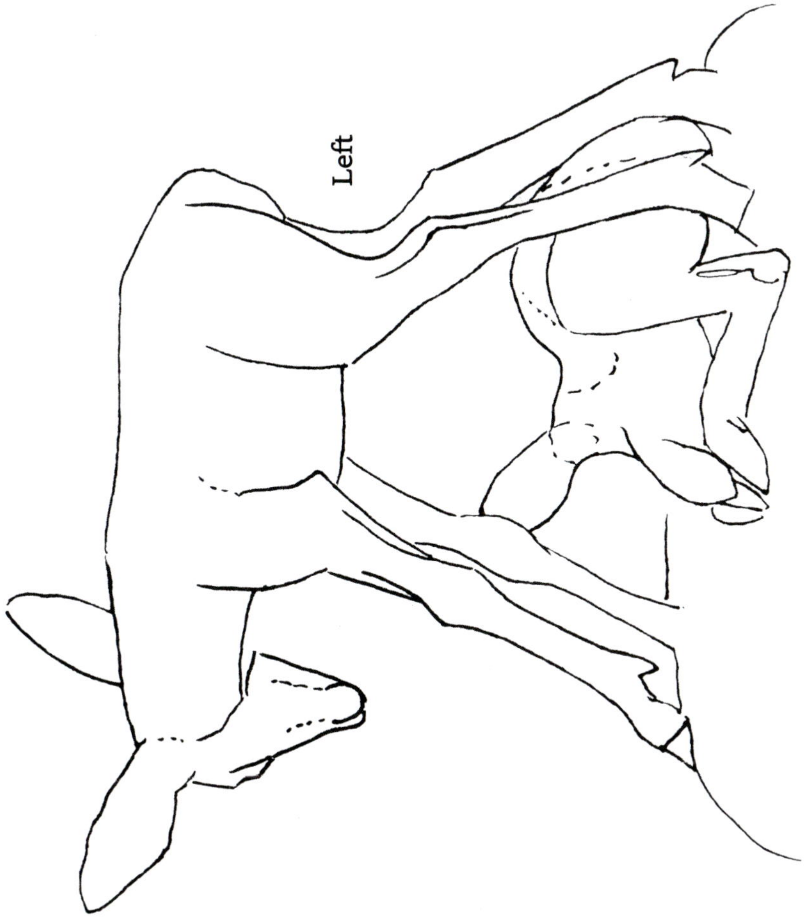

Back

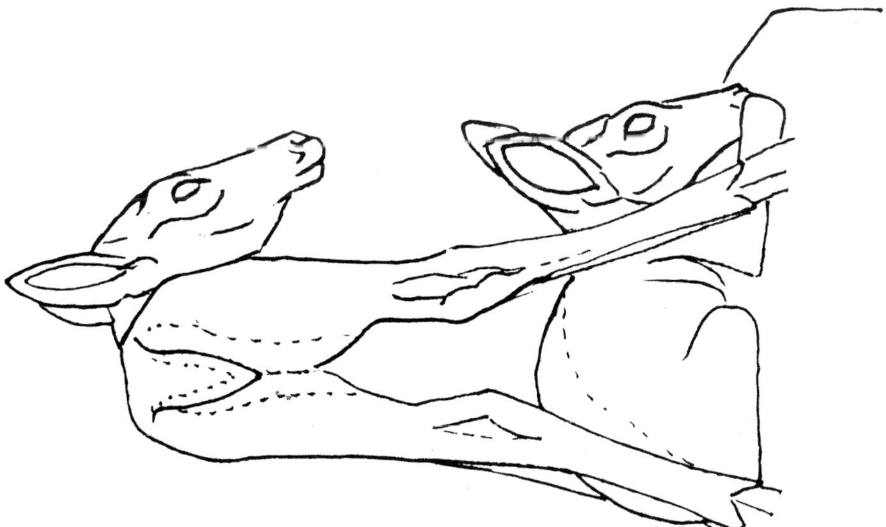

DOE AND FAWN

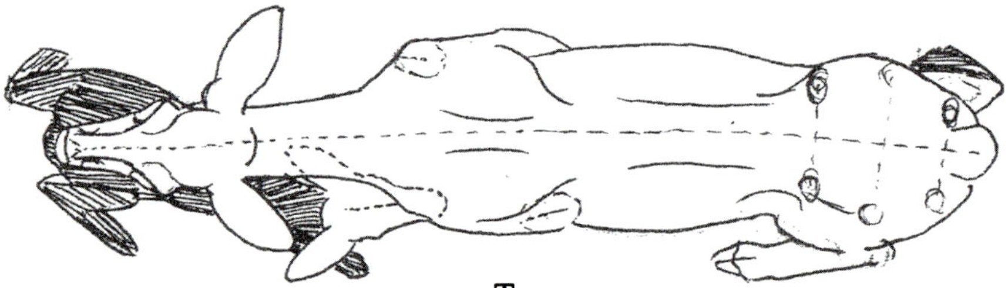

Top

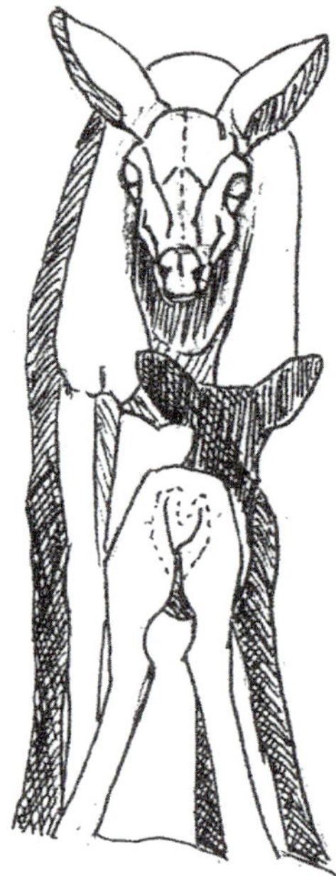

Front

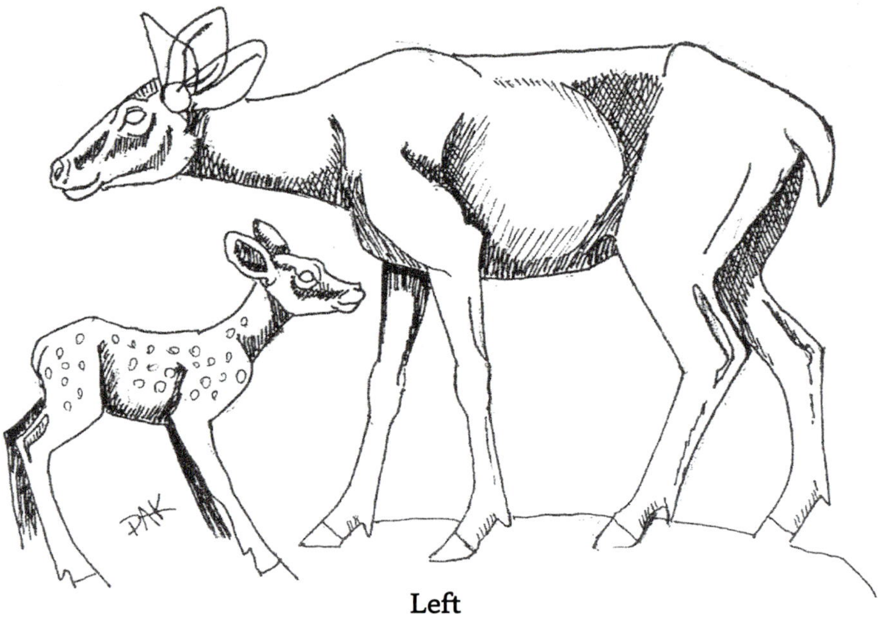

Left

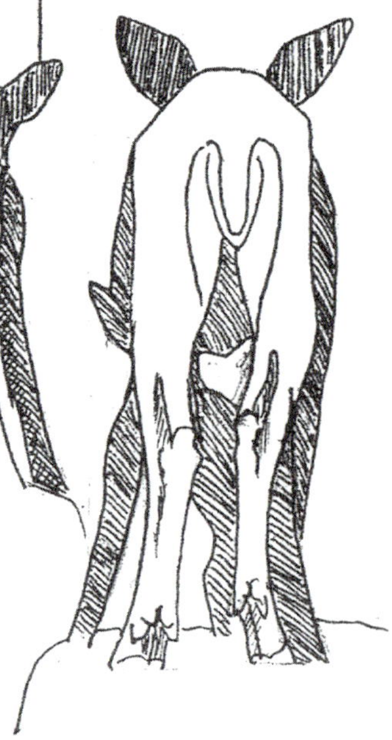

Back

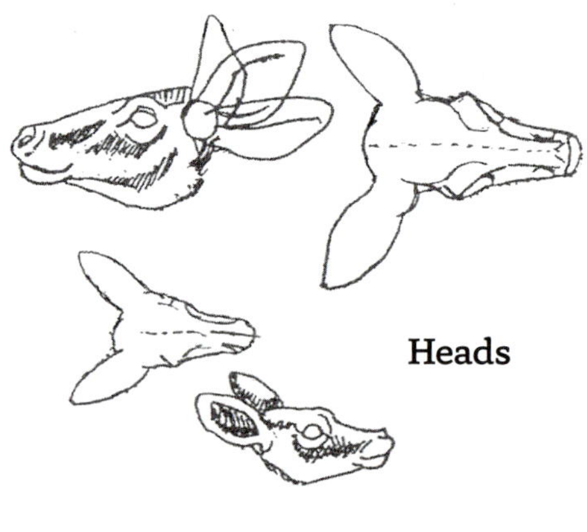

Heads

Patterns are labeled from the point-of-view of the doe.

FAWN

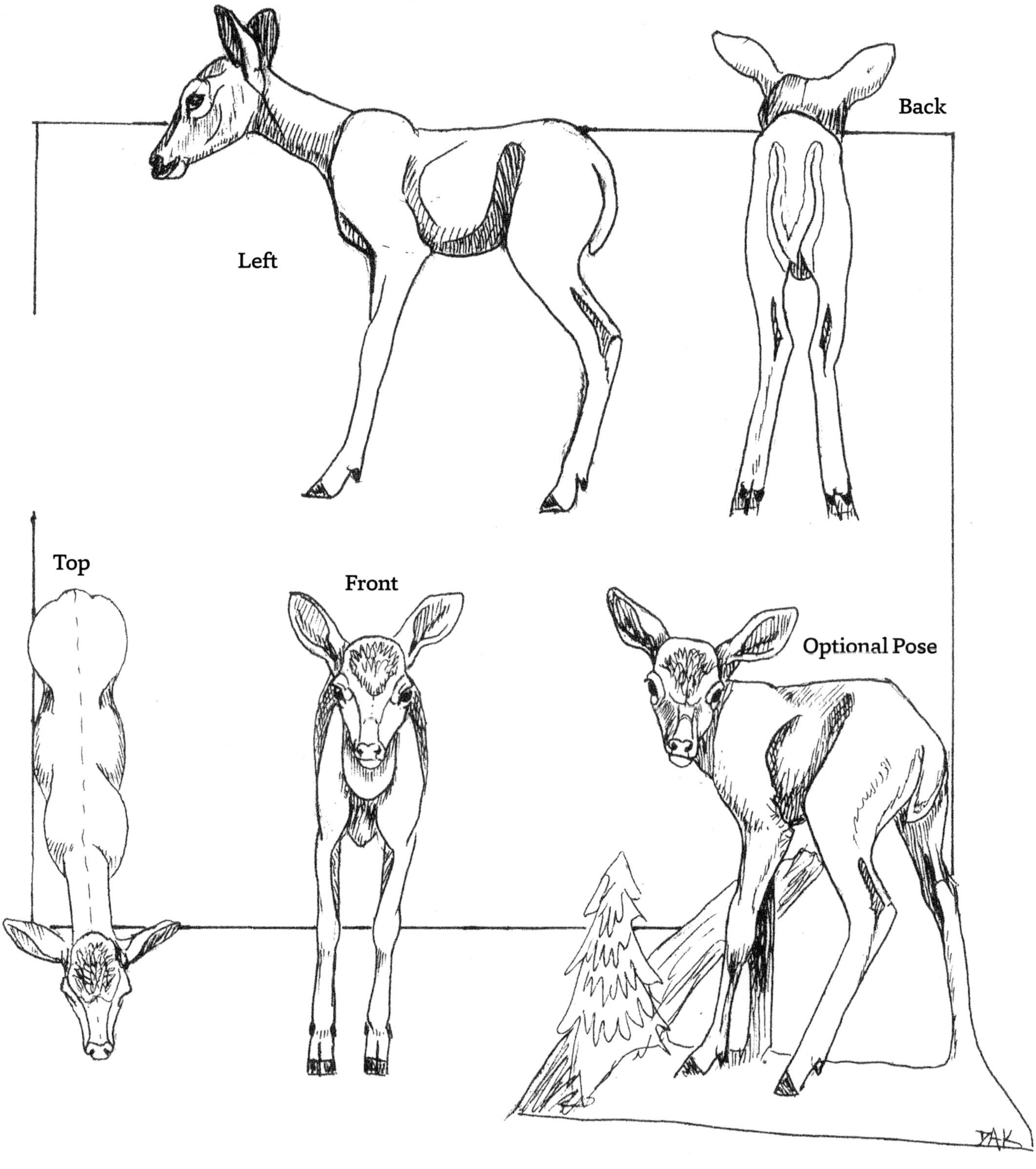

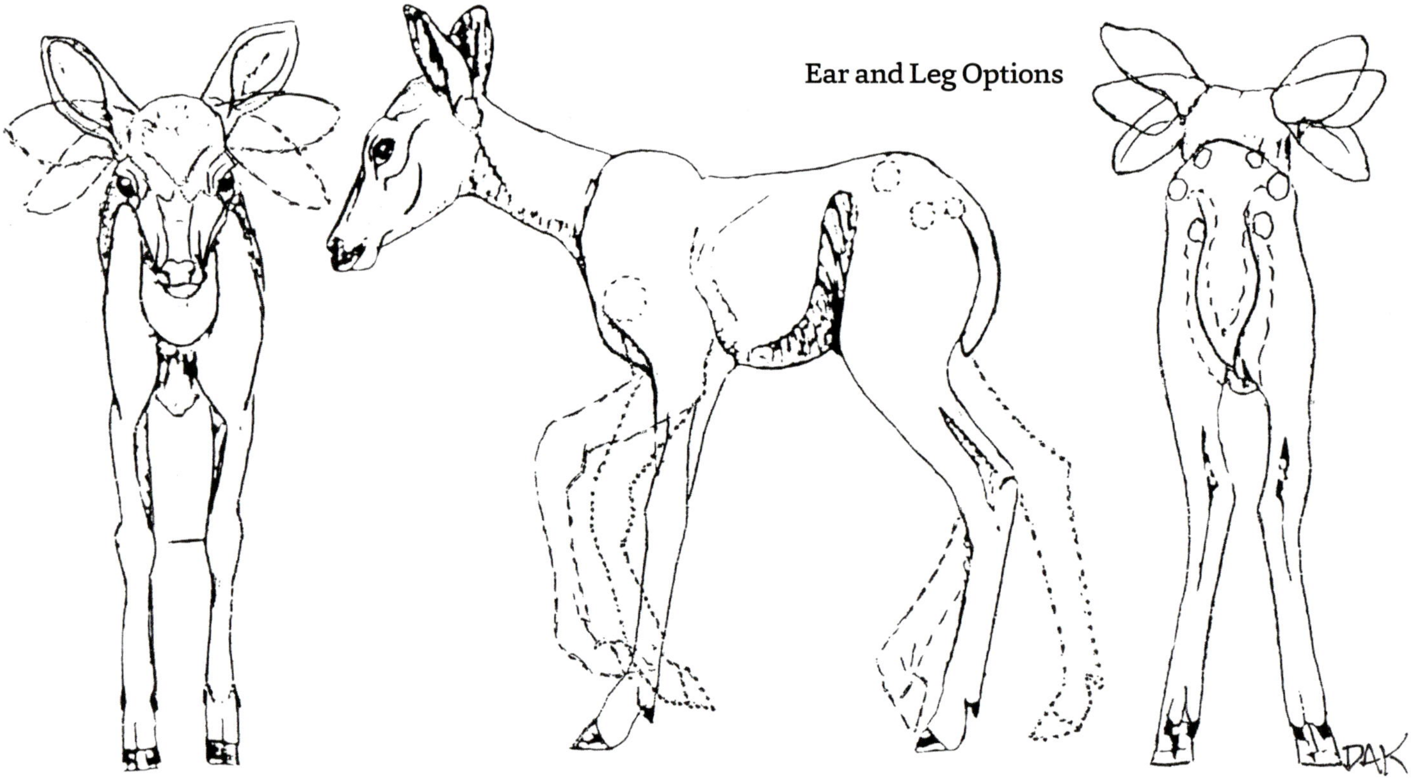

Ear and Leg Options

Appendix

On the following pages, you will find drawings and reference photos detailing deer anatomy, movement, stances, and features, along with some tips for carving particular deer features. The tips for carving deer features show how to use hand tools and power tools to carve deer eyes, noses, mouths, and ears. The steps and carving order are the same for both hand and power carving, you just use different tools for each method.

Use these drawings, study sketches, and reference photos to help you carve the projects in this book, redesign the patterns, or to create your own. Whether you'd like to make small changes to a pattern, like turning the deer's head, or complex changes, like altering the animal's pose, these guidelines will help you mold your own ideas.

CARVING SPECIFIC FEATURES

Deer Eyes

FRONT **SIDE**

1 Draw the eye, lid, and lower lid. Use a V-tool to cut along these lines. If using rotary tools, use a bud or flame tip.

2 For the corners of the eye (the tear duct and outer part of the eye), use a knife to make an inverted pyramid on each colored corner. If using rotary tools, use a bud or flame tip.

3 To ensure the eyeball is in its socket and rounded, undercut with a knife point on the eyeball under the eyelid. If using rotary tools, use a bud or flame tip.

4 To woodburn, use a skew or microskew tip and utilize a stab/pull motion in the direction of the fur around the eyeball. Burnish the eyeball with the flat of the skew tip.

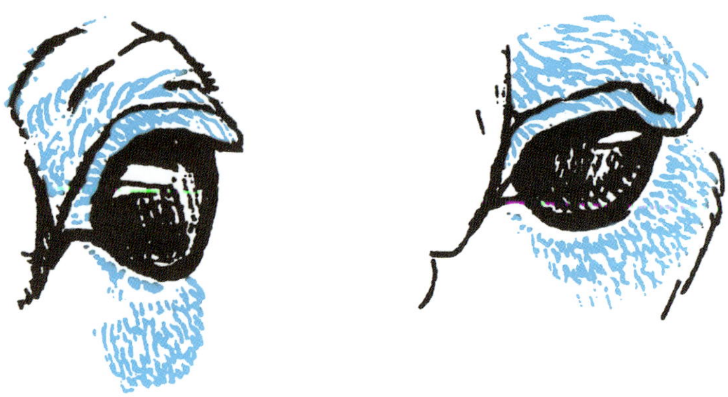

Deer Nose and Mouth

FRONT | SIDE

1 Draw the silhouettes of the front and side of the nose and mouth area and mouth. Draw in the nostrils. Cut along the lines of the mouth and the edges of the nostrils with a V-tool. If using rotary tools, use a flame or bud tip.

2 Use a 3/8" (10mm) #9 gouge or ball tip in a rotary tool on the inside of each nostril. This will give the illusion of breathing. Gouge the cleft between the nostrils to show the flex point, and gouge the soft tissue behind the nostrils. Refer to the colored sections on the sketch.

3 Use a detail knife, or, if using rotary tools, a cylinder, bud, or flame tip, to undercut below the muzzle to make the chin thinner. The muzzle should look like it hangs over the chin.

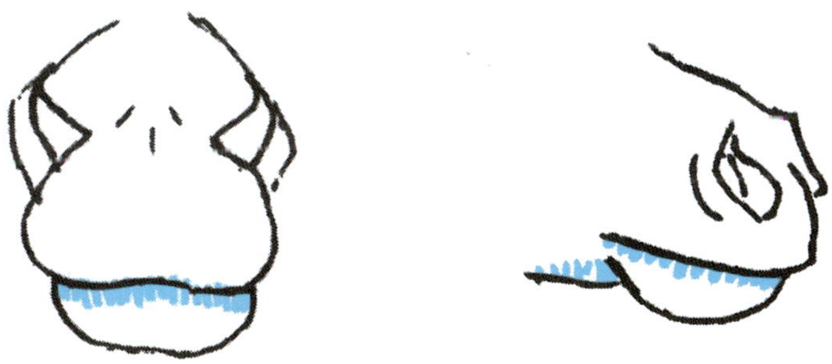

4 Woodburn with a skew or microskew tip in the direction of the fur. Burnish the nosepad with a writing tip. This will give it a nice texture.

Deer Ears

FRONT SIDE

1 Draw the front and side silhouettes of the ear. Use a ⅜" (10mm) #6 gouge to trim it to shape. If using rotary tools, use a flame or bud tip.

2 Draw a line of cartilage roll. Use a V-tool to cut along the line. If using rotary tools, use a small rotary ball or bud tip. This will keep the edges of the ear from splitting.

3 Use gouges to remove the inside of the ear to the cartilage roll. If using rotary tools, use a ball tip.

4 Woodburn with a skew tip in the direction of the fur. You can also use a microskew tip.

DEER DETAILS AND ANATOMY

Deer Skeleton

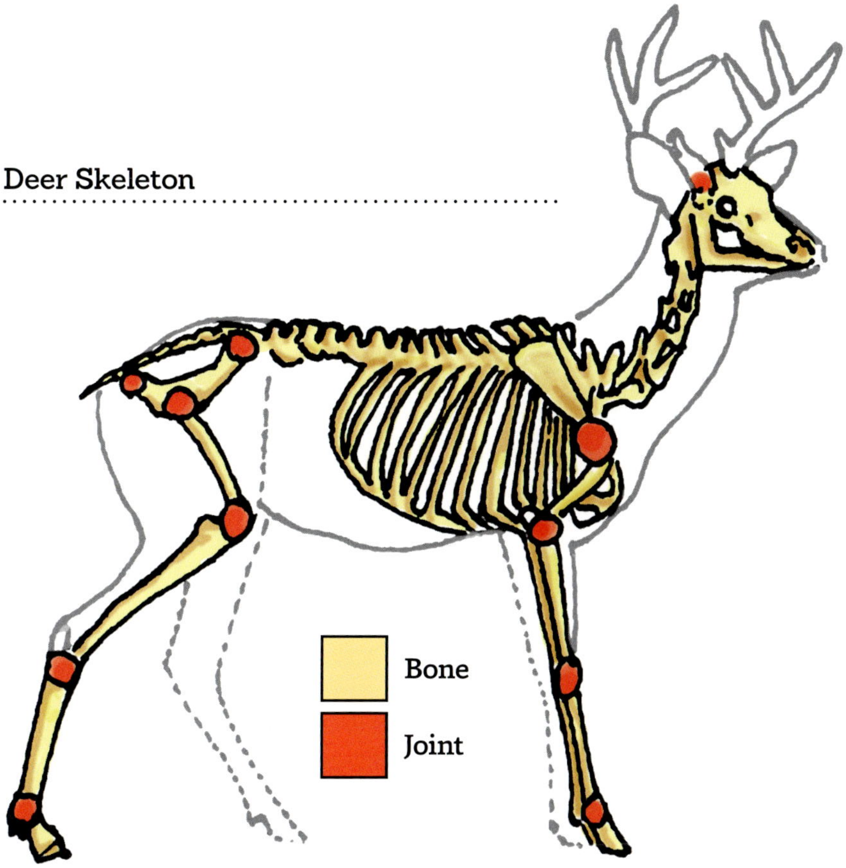

Deer Muscle Structure

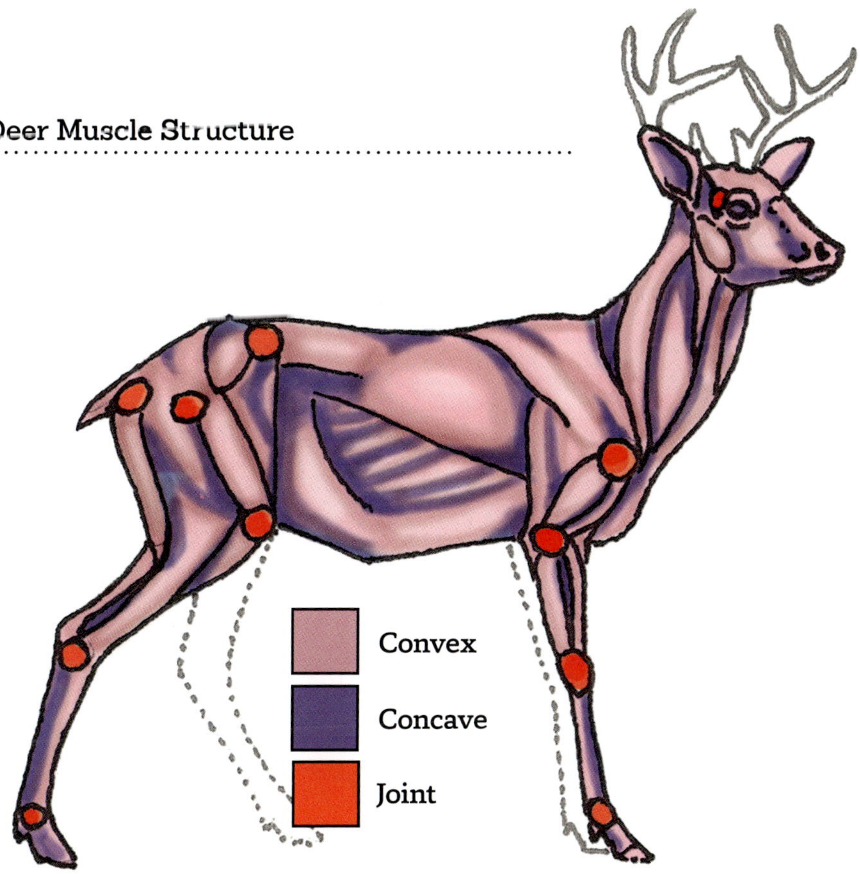

Ear Anatomy
Cartilage connected to the skull is located above the pivot point of the jaw area where it fits into the skull (see the red shaded circles). This area stays connected to the skull, but turns the ears so the animal can be on constant alert for danger. The ear itself is pear-shaped with a hollowed-out center. The pear sits on the sphere.

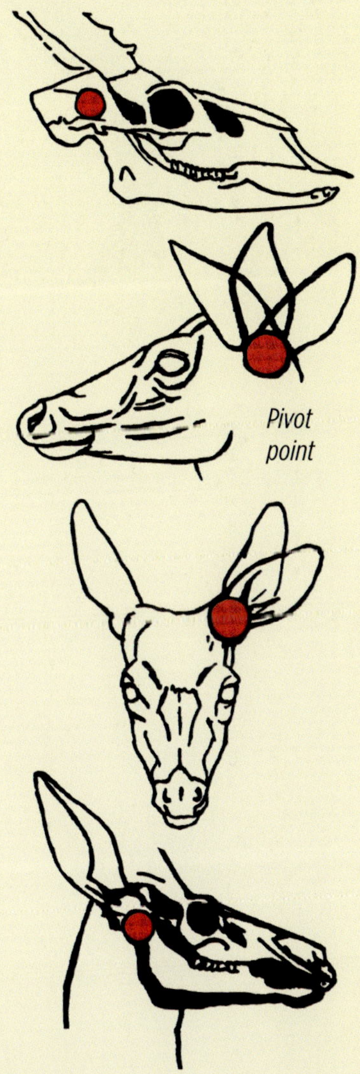

The deer lacks upper front teeth; it has a tough pad instead.

Deer Coloring

Deer Hair Tract

DEER STANCES

Walking Front View

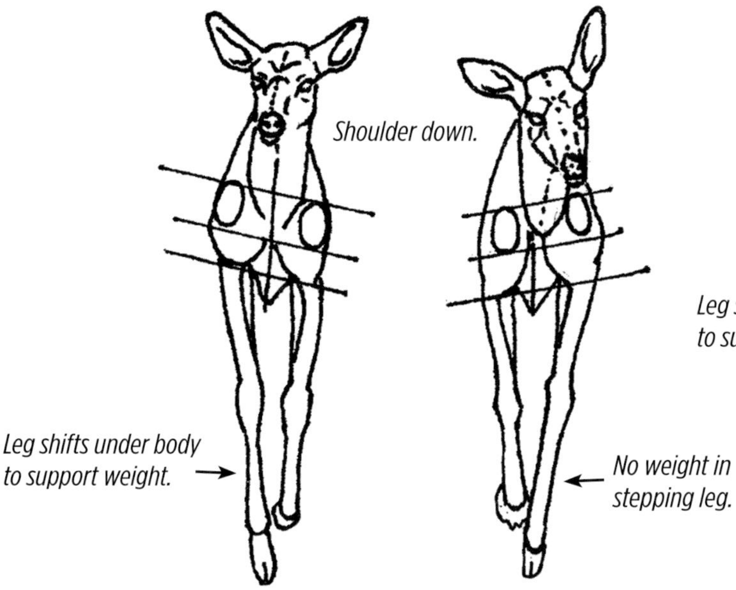

Walking Rear View

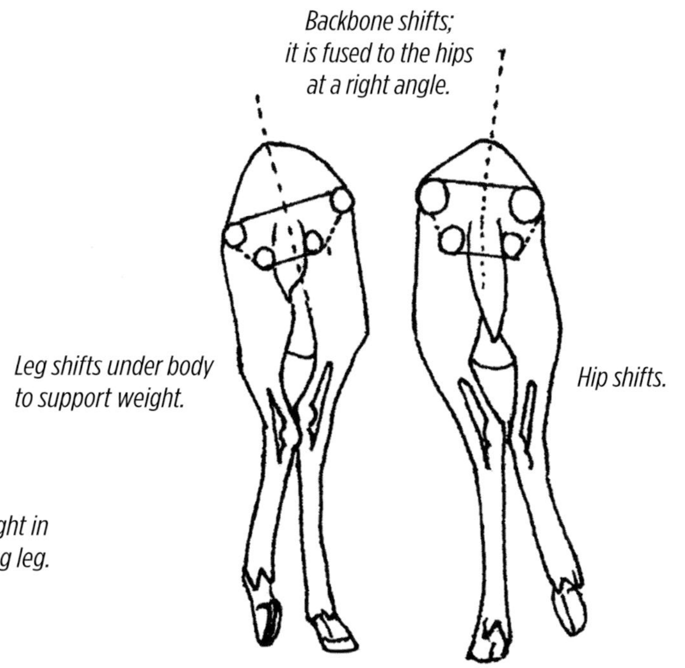

Walking Top View

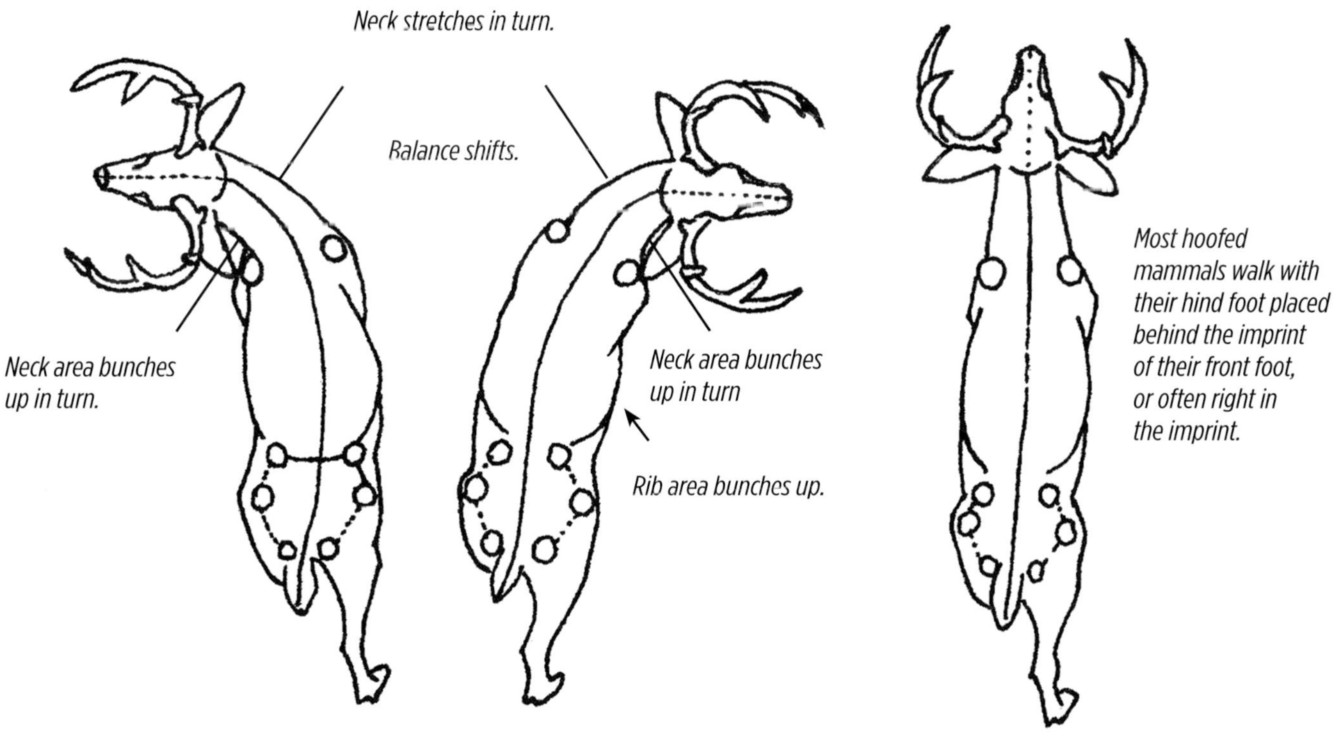

Deer Feet

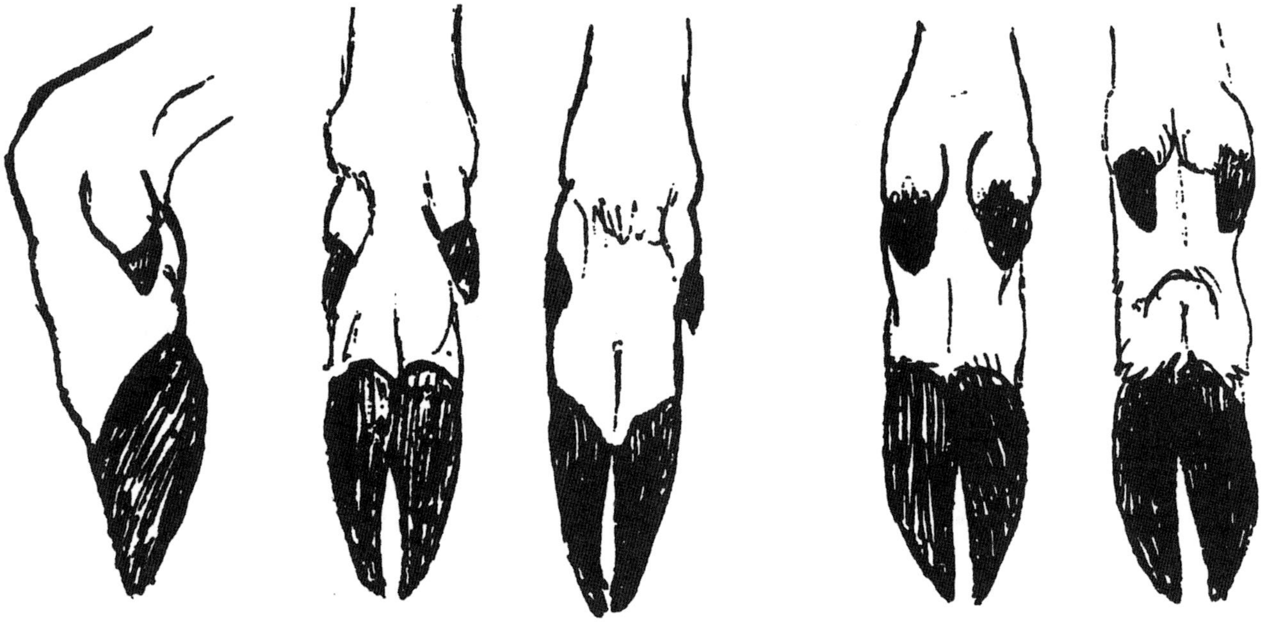

Side | Bottom | Top | Front Foot | Hind Foot

Notice the dewclaws are farther from the hooves on the hind foot.

White-tailed deer

Deer running

Dewclaws will show on cloven hoofed animals when running.

Toes will be splayed.

Back hoof fits into front hoof print.

Drag marks will appear in deep snow when walking.

STUDY SKETCHES

On the following pages are a few additional detail sketches to get you close to the deer by showing its head and face up close. Note the details of the antlers, hair growth patterns, ears, and eyes. Try sketching your own deer carving pattern with the high level of detail shown here to prepare yourself for your real carving.

Nose

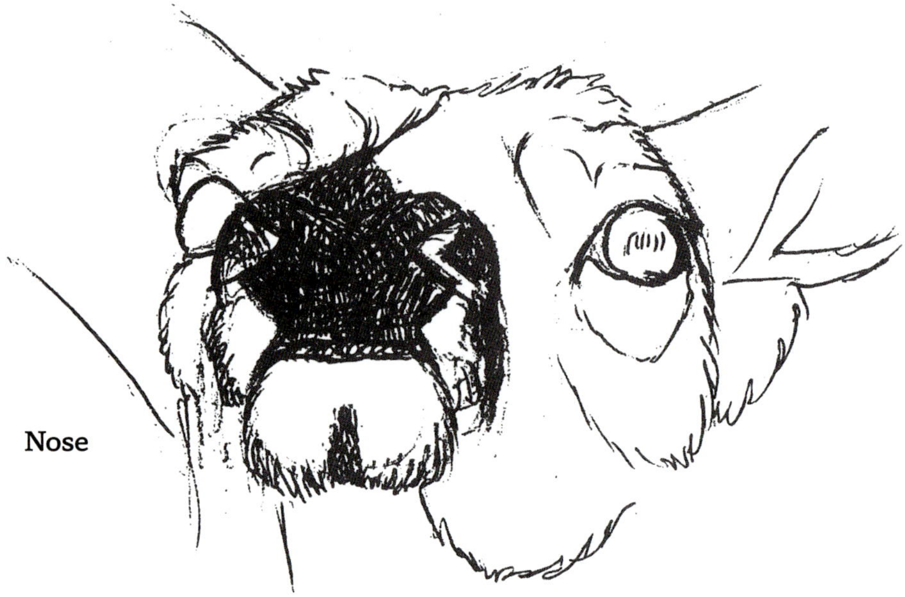

Antler

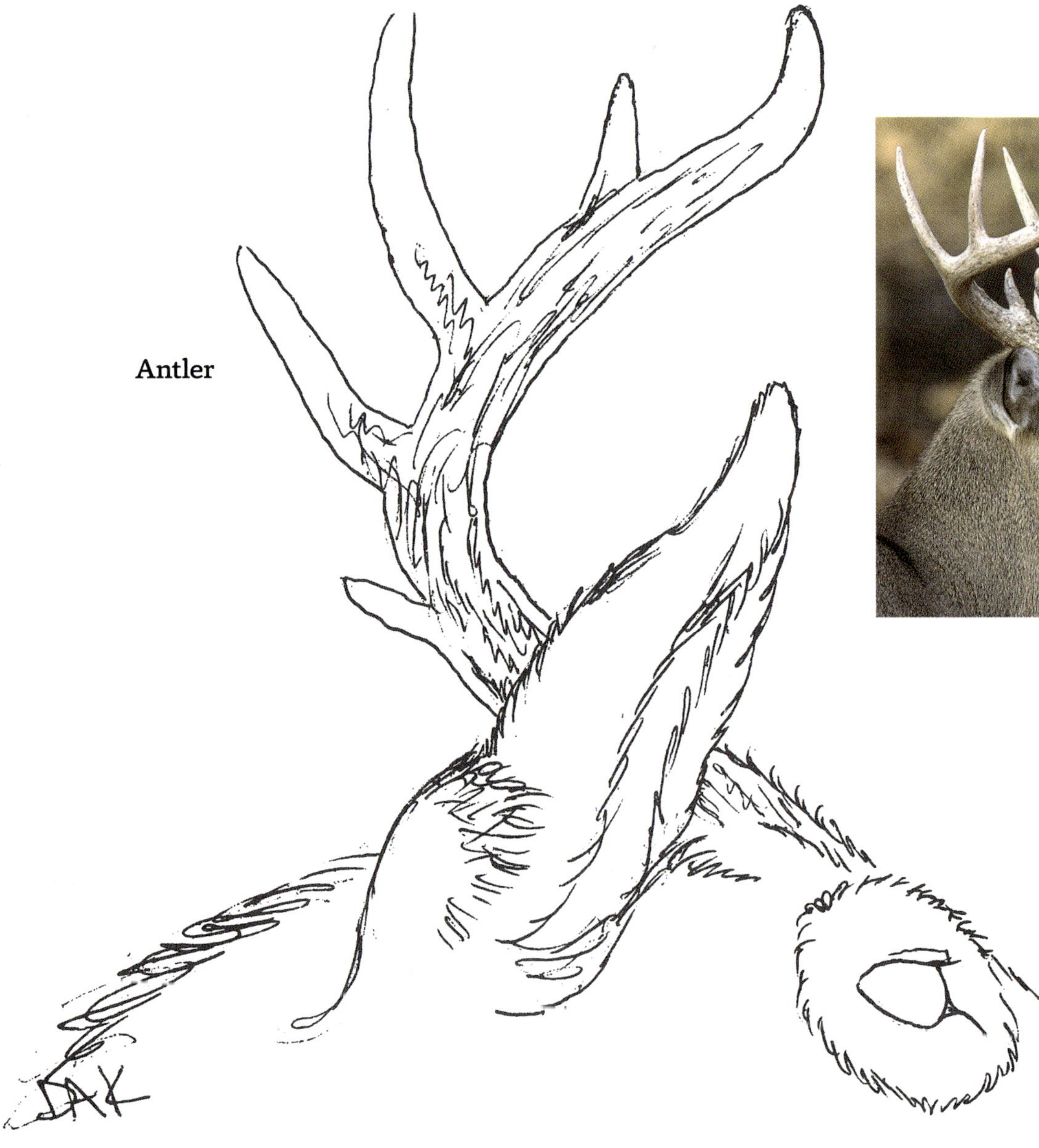

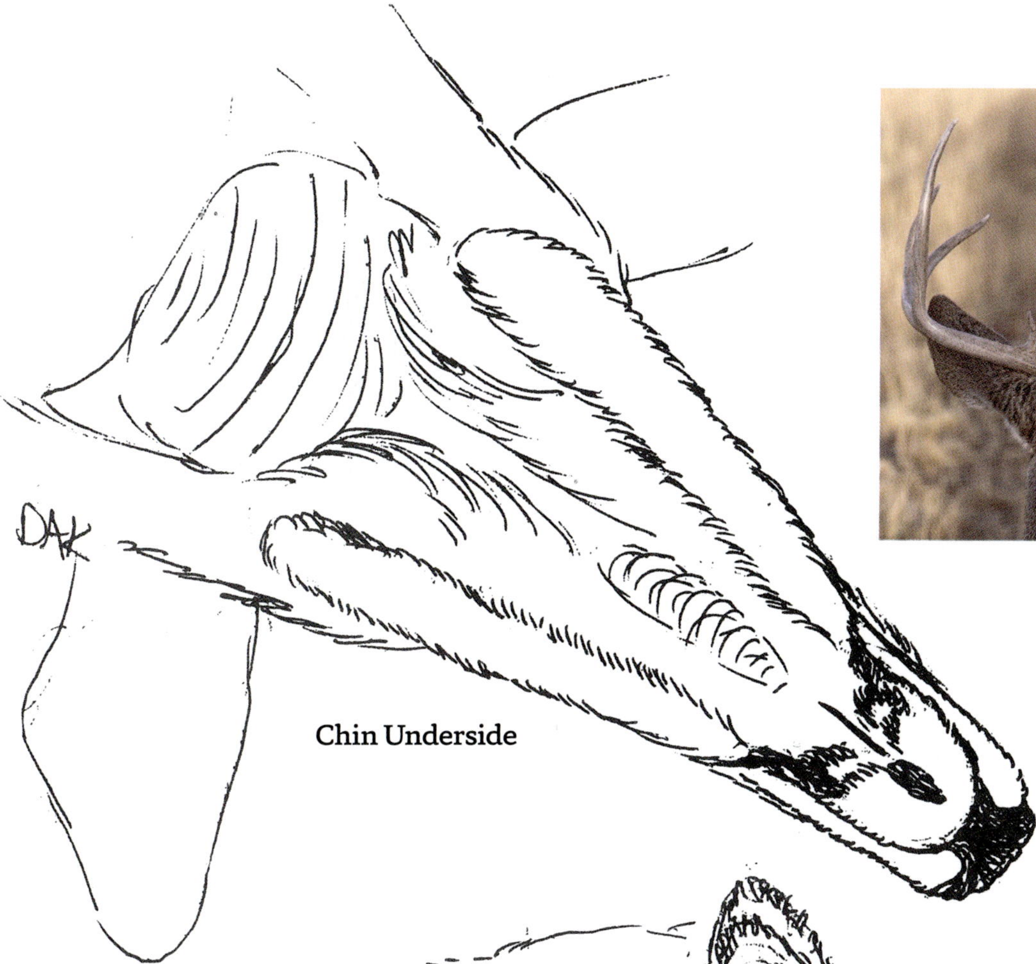

Chin Underside

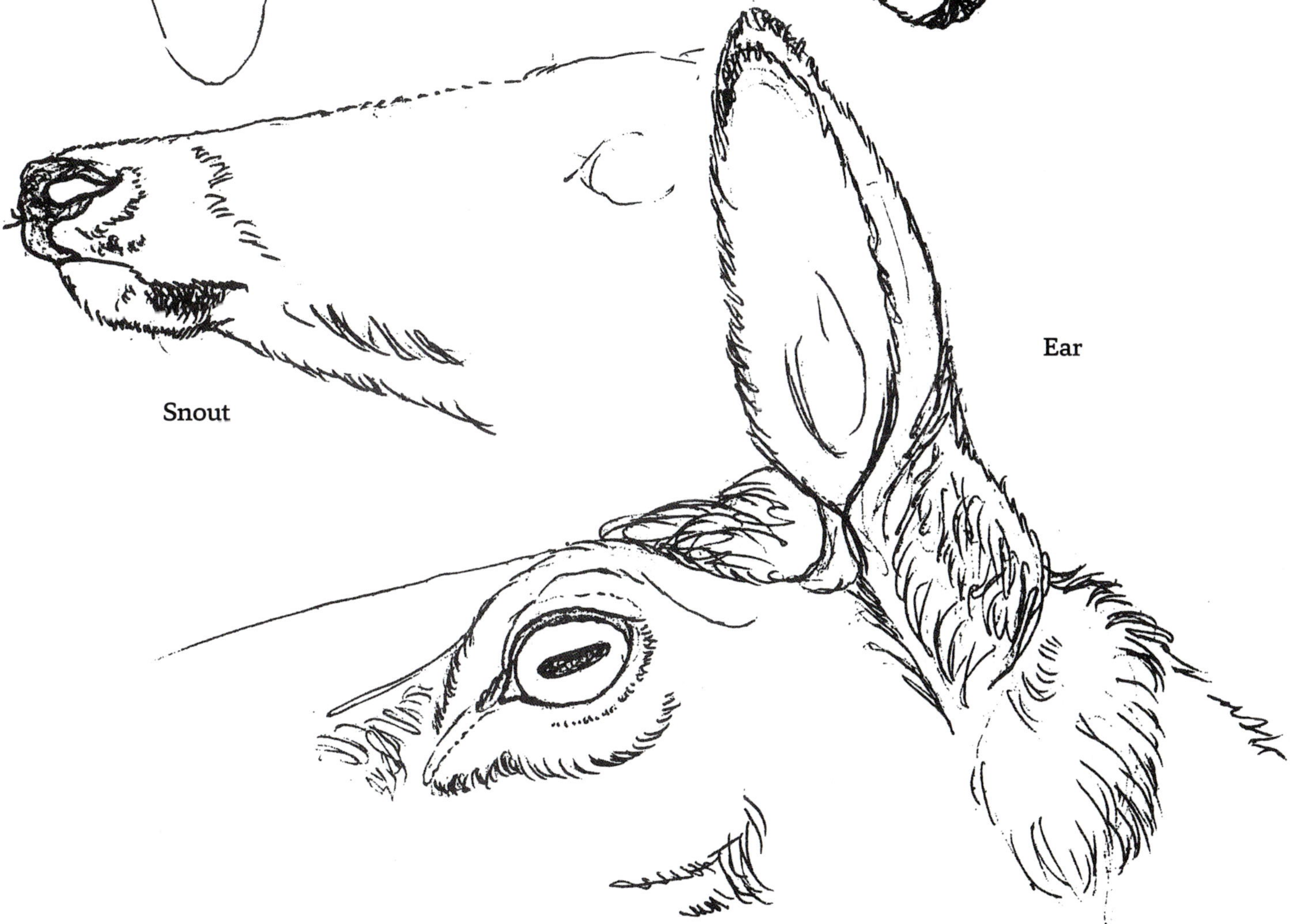

Snout

Ear

REFERENCE PHOTOS

Bucks

Bucks Fighting

Antlers in Velvet

Does

Fawns

Tails